TABLE OF CONTENTS

PAGE 7

PAGE 14

PAGE 26

ABOUT THE AUTHOR

After graduating from Concordia College in Moorhead, Minnesota, Gail taught English in the Minneapolis public schools. A gift of quilt blocks made from old worn fabrics, a magazine article, and a 1963 purchase of a needlework book by Rose Wilder Lane were the beginnings of her quiltmaking journey.

Gail learned about quilts and quiltmaking by reading books. Her study of quiltmaking grew coincidentally with raising three active daughters. Winning a sweepstakes award at a local fair led to teaching adult education quilting classes. In 1982 Gail was certified as a national quilting teacher by the Embroiderer's Guild of America. Her quilts have been shown locally and juried into regional quilt shows.

In *Starry Nights: 3 Great Quilts, 3 Great Techniques*, Gail gives quick-piecing instructions and adds her own methods for rotary-cutting short-cuts.

Gail and her husband live 36 miles from the Canadian border in a small town on the prairies of Montana near where her parents raised wheat and where her grandparents homesteaded.

The Perfect Miter

The perfect miter technique begins with a working border length to provide ease for the "turn of the cloth" when mitering. The working border is trimmed after it is sewn. As an alternative method, you can pre-cut the miter to fit, as described on page 4.

★ The "working length" of a border is the side of the quilt or square (unfinished), plus the unfinished width of the cut border at each end. *Example (Fig. 1):* Cut a 2" (unfinished) border for a 4½" (unfinished) square, (2" + 4½" + 2" = 8½"). Be accurate. The miter seams depend on evenly cut borders.

★ Transfer the four working-length border strips to the ironing board. Mark the center of each strip within the seam allowance.

★ To find the miter placement, measure the side of the unfinished quilt or square. Subtract 1" from the measurement. Divide the result by two. For the 4½" square, 4½" minus 1" = 3½" divided by two = 1¾". For the 4½" square, place a mark 1¾" to the right and 1¾" to the left of center. Draw a line across the width of the border strips at the marks (Fig. 2).

★ *Note:* When sewing several bordered squares, a template can be used to mark the center and the distances to the right and left of center. In the example, the template would be a rectangle 2" wide by 3½" in length with a mark at the center (Fig. 3).

★ Fold the upper-right and upper-left corners down at the drawn lines. The folds form flaps like "collie ears" (Fig. 4). Press. (The border ends will extend below the bottom edge of the strip.) Repeat the process for the remaining three border strips.

2" + 4½" square + 2" = 8½"

Fig. 1. Cut border 8½" for a 4½" square.

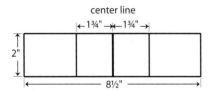

center line

Fig. 2. Mark miter placement.

center mark

Fig. 3. Template is faster and more accurate.

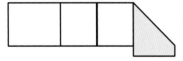

Fig. 4. Press diagonal creases to establish the miter line.

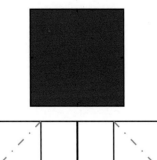

Fig. 5. Match center of the square and border strip.

★ *Note:* By pressing the diagonal crease to establish the miter line, an allowance for the turn of the cloth at the seam has been made. Do not cut away the fabric that extends beyond the creased miter lines until the final pressing of the square.

★ Match the centers of the borders to the centers of the sides of the square. (Fig. 5).

★ Sew the border strip to the square, beginning one stitch in from the pressed miter line. Sew to within one stitch of the miter crease on the opposite side of the square (Fig. 6). Next, sew the border on the opposite side of the square, followed by the remaining two borders.

★ Fold the bordered square in half diagonally, right sides together. Open the flaps. Perfectly align the blunt ends of the strips and pin. Finger press all seam allowances toward the square.

★ Sew the miters in the crease, while keeping the blunt ends of the strips even (Fig. 7).

★ While the square is still folded diagonally, cut off the fabric that extends beyond the crease, leaving ¼" seam allowance (Fig. 8).

★ Press the mitered seams clockwise and the center square flat (Fig. 9).

★ You have a bordered square with perfect miters (Fig. 10).

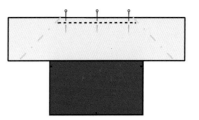

Fig. 6. Sew border strips to square.

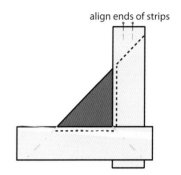

Fig. 7. Sew the miters in the crease.

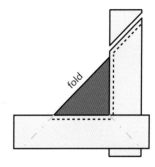

Fig. 8. Trim, leaving ¼" seam allowance.

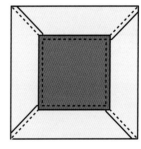

Fig. 9. Press mitered seams clockwise and center square flat.

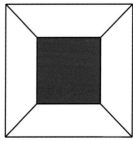

Fig. 10. Bordered square, with perfect miter.

The Perfect Pre-cut Miter

The pre-cut mitered border is the most convenient border to use for patches or blocks. The seam allowances for the mitered corners are included in the pre-cut border.

★ The length of the pre-cut mitered border, unlike the working border, is the finished square plus the width of the unfinished border plus ⅛" at each end. *Example:* To border a 4" square (finished) with a 1½" border (unfinished), add 1½" (border width) at each end of the border to allow for the seam allowances at the mitered corners. Add ⅛" at each end to allow for the turn of the cloth. Thus, ⅛" + 1½" + 4" + 1½" + ⅛" = 7¼" (Fig. 11).

★ To make a template (Fig. 12) for the border in the example, fold the upper corners of a 1½" x 7¼" paper rectangle down to meet the base of the rectangle to create the 45-degree angle for mitering the borders. Cut off the triangles at each end. The template includes the seam allowances for mitering. Paste the paper pattern to template plastic and cut out. Use the template to pre-cut the borders. Sew the pre-cut borders and the miters with a ¼" seam allowance.

★ *Note:* You can stabilize the squares to be bordered with spray sizing. When cutting the borders, alternate the base of the template between the top and the bottom of the strip.

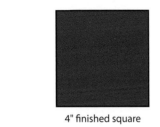

4" finished square

Fig. 11. Figure the length of the pre-cut mitered border

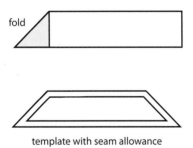

fold

template with seam allowance

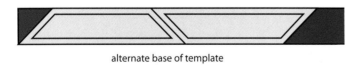

alternate base of template

Fig. 12. Make a template

The Easy-Eight Mitered Star

The Easy-eight is a four-patch, cut-easy-sew-easy star that is trouble-free. It requires only the pre-cut-miter and the corner-square techniques for instant success.

★ To find the size of the square needed, determine the finished size of the block. Divide the finished size in half and add 1½" for seam allowances and cutting ease.

★ Sew pre-cut borders to the square and miter the corners (Fig. 13).

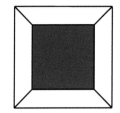

Fig. 13. Sew pre-cut borders to the square and miter corners.

The Easy-Eight Mitered Star

EXAMPLES

6" square

Finished size	Cut Square
6" divided by 2 = 3" + 1½" =	4½"

10" square

Finished size	Cut Square
10" divided by 2 = 5" + 1½" =	6½"

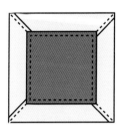

Fig. 14. Press frame seams clockwise and center square flat.

★ Turn the bordered square to the wrong side (Fig. 14). Using the measurement for the inside cuts from the Easy-Eight Cutting Chart, place the ruler on a seam joining the border to the square. Align the ruler's horizontal lines with the seam lines of adjacent borders. Cut across the center of the square, dividing the square (Fig. 15).

★ Repeat the measuring and cutting for the opposite side of the square. A scrap will remain in the center. Cut each piece again by aligning the ruler with the seams, as before. There will be scraps between these pieces also (Fig. 16).

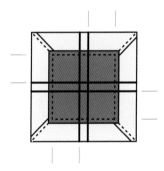

Fig. 15. Measure inside cuts from the seam line.

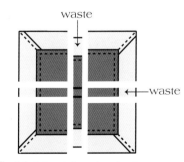

Fig. 16. Cut and discard waste pieces.

Fig. 13–16. Easy-eight Mitered Star

Fig. 17. Squares cut from background fabric, the same width as border.

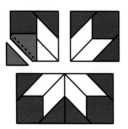

Fig. 18. Sew square on diagonals parallel to the mitered seams.

Fig. 19. Sew four quarters together.

Fig. 17–19. Easy-Eight Mitered Star

★ On one of the pieces, place a square of background fabric (cut the same size as the border width) (Fig. 17).

★ Sew the background square to the piece with a diagonal seam, corner to corner. The diagonal seam across the square should be parallel to the mitered seams.

★ Cut off the waste triangles, leaving a ¼" seam allowance. Repeat for the other side of the piece (Fig. 18).

★ Repeat for the other three quarters and press the units.

★ Turn the four units so the mitered corners are in the center of the star block. Sew the block as a four-patch, magically producing the Easy-Eight Mitered Star (Fig. 19).

Easy-Eight Cutting Chart

Finished Star Block	Working Square Cut Size (½ finished star + 1½")	Background Squares (¼ finished star + ½")	Pre-cut Border (block + ¼")	Seamline Cuts* (¼ finished
6"	4½"	2"	2" x 8¼"	1¾"
8"	5½"	2½"	2½" x 10¼"	2¼"
10"	6½"	3"	3" x 12¼"	2¾"
12"	7½"	3½"	3½" x 14¼"	3¼"

* Measure from border seams on the wrong side.

FALLING STARS, 36" x 36", made by Pat Feeney and quilted by Pat Meldrum

FALLING STARS

Cube Lattice Blocks, 8"

★ ★ ★

**Easy-Eight
Star points
p. 9**

**FALLING STARS, 36" x 36", made by Pat Feeney
and quilted by Pat Meldrum**

		Cut strips selvage to selvage. Be sure to label all your pieces with their cut sizes.			
Materials	**Yards.**	**First cut**		**Second cut**	
Scraps		⅛ yard each of 11 different fabrics for the star points and pieced border 1 leftovers, vary the hue and intensity		12 squares	3⅜"
				2 squares	1½"
Dark Blue	2⅛	1 strip	7½"	2 rectangles	7½" x 15½"
		2 strips	5½"	11 squares	5½"
		1 strip	4½"	2 rectangles	4½" x 8½"
		leftovers		2 rectangles	4½" x 2½"
				2 squares	3⅜"
		6 strips	2½"	88 squares	2½"
Border One		3 strips	1½"		
Border Two		4 strips	2½"		
Backing	1⅛	1 panel	40½" x 40½"		
Binding	½ (included in dark blue yardage)				
Batting		42" x 42"			

Fig. 20. Cut using 2½" x 10¼" template.

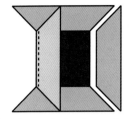

Fig. 21. Sew the borders to the square.

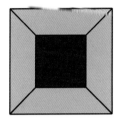

Fig. 22. Sew pre-cut borders to the square and miter corners.

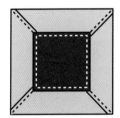

Fig. 23. Press seam allowances clockwise.

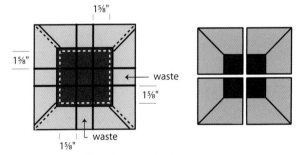

Fig. 24. Cut the bordered squares into four star-point units.

Fig. 25. Sew 2½" squares in opposite corners parallel to seamline to make star-points.

Fig. 20–25. Easy-Eight Star Points

For the FALLING STARS wallhanging, use the Easy-eight technique (pages 5-6) to make a four-patch star from a bordered square. The Easy-eight technique provides rotary-cut, pre-pieced units instead of individual parallelograms for the star points, which makes the Easy-eight a speed technique.

The Cube Lattice block, when pieced edge to edge, forms a repetitive star design. However, in FALLING STARS, whole and partial stars make the design.

The stars are made from ⅛ yard each of 11 different fabrics that range from green to gold to orange. The colors vary in hue and intensity.

TEMPLATE CONSTRUCTION

The borders for the 5½" dark blue squares can be pre-cut. Make a wedge-shaped template by drawing and cutting a 2½" x 10¼" paper rectangle. Cut 45-degree angles at each end. Paste the paper template to template plastic and cut out the template. Cut a 2½" strip from each star point fabric and use the wedge template to cut four borders from each fabric (Fig. 20). Alternate the base of the template from edge to edge along the strips.

EASY-EIGHT STAR POINTS

★ Sew the pre-cut wedge borders to the 5½" dark blue squares. Sew opposite sides when applying the first two strips for an easy application (Fig. 21).

★ Miter the corners (Fig. 22). Trim the protruding tips from the mitered strips. Press the center square flat. Press the corner seam allowances clockwise (Fig. 23).

★ Turn the bordered squares face down. Place the 2¼" line of the cutting ruler on the seam line that joins the border to the dark blue square. Slice across the bordered square (Fig. 24).

★ Rotate bordered square to cut from each side. There will be some waste between the units. Cut all 11 bordered squares into accurate units (Fig. 24).

★ Place two 2½" squares face down on each of the units. Sew the diagonals of the squares from the outside edge of the border to the inside edge of the applied squares (Fig. 25).

★ Cut away the waste triangles. Fold back the applied squares to complete the star points. (Two are extra.)

BORDERED RECTANGLES

A pieced border is sewn to the large 7½" x 15½" blue rectangles that appear at the lower left half and at the upper right half of the quilt.

★ Cut two dark blue 3⅜" squares and 14 colored 3⅜" squares. Sew 16 half-squares. Arrange the half-squares into two horizontal rows of five half-squares ending with a blue/color half-square. Arrange the remaining half-squares into two vertical rows of two half-squares. Begin each vertical row with a blue/color half square. Sew the half-squares into four rows (Fig. 26).

★ Cut a 1½" strip along the middle (lengthwise) of the horizontal and vertical rows. Sew a 1½" dark blue strip to the blue end of the horizontal rows. Sew a 1½" dark blue strip to the blue end of the vertical rows and a 1½" colored square to the opposite end.

★ Complete by sewing the horizontal and the vertical strips to two adjacent sides of the 7½" x 15½" dark blue rectangles (Fig. 27).

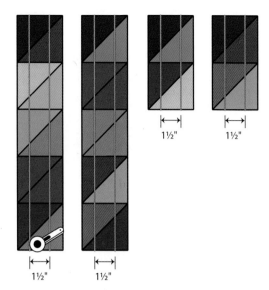

Fig. 26. Cut 1½" strip from the middle of each half-square strip.

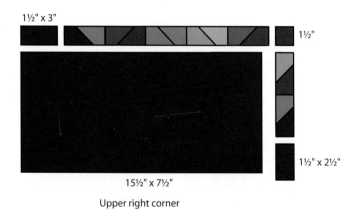

Upper right corner

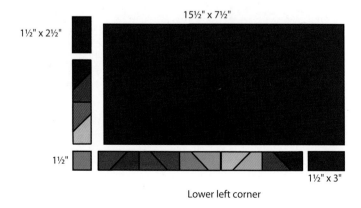

Lower left corner

Fig. 27. Bordered rectangles upper right and lower left corners

QUILT ASSEMBLY

★ Arrange 21 star point units for the left half of the wallhanging according to the quilt assembly diagram. Repeat the layout for the right half. Turn the right half upside down. (The left half of the wallhanging ends with the multicolored strip. The right half begins with the multicolored strip.)

BORDER

Cut four blue 2½" x 37½" pre-cut borders. Center and sew the borders to the wallhanging. Sew the pre-cut mitered borders at each corner.

FINISHING

Layer the quilt with batting and a backing, quilt the layers together. Bind the raw edges of the quilt with 2" continuous, double-fold bias binding.

Fig. 28. Quilt assembly

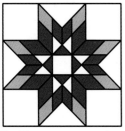

Fig. 29. Northumberland Star

Fig. 30. Union Star

Fig. 31. Liberty Star

Fig. 32. Dove in the Window

Fig. 29–32. Blocks using strip-pieced diamonds or parallelograms

Fig. 33. Lone Star

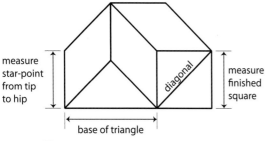

measure star-point from tip to hip

diagonal

measure finished square

base of triangle

Finished square x 1.414 + 1¼" = size of square to cut base triangle.

Fig. 34. Base triangles for Lone Star blocks

Star points can be diamond- or parallelogram-shaped. Parallelograms, like diamonds, have two parallel sets of sides, but their sides are not equal in length, and the widths between the parallel sides are not equal. Like diamonds, parallelograms can be sewn and cut by using strip piecing.

When multiple fabric strips are sewn together into layers and then cut, several equal-sized sets of diamonds or parallelograms are produced. By planning the layering of the strata by the number of strips, strip width, and color, different designs can be made.

Examples of strip piecing to make diamond or parallelogram star points include the Northumberland Star (diamonds) (Fig. 29) and the Union Star (parallelograms) (Fig. 30). Layered strips can be sewn to make patterns within individual diamonds, such as the three-stripe Liberty Star (Fig. 31). Strata can also be sewn to make figurative patterns like Dove in the Window (Fig. 32).

The Lone Star, like the Eight-Pointed Star block, is an octagon-based star. It is sewn using multiples of 45-degree diamonds rather than eight individual diamonds. Lone Stars are sewn using the strip method to create rows of stars.

The size of the Lone Star may be designed to fit within 54", 60", or 76" squares, the largest squares that fit the double, queen, or king mattress tops. A common means of enlarging the Lone Star, however, is to add an additional row to the star point, changing a five diamond/five row star point into a six diamond/six row star point. For example, when using a 2" diamond, the increase of one diamond enlarges the Lone Star by 5¾".

Differences in quilt sizes also depend on the design. The Lone Star set within a square with four squares and four base triangles between star points is much smaller than the same Lone Star in a Rolling Star setting when the eight squares between star points are incorporated into the design.

To design a Lone Star (Fig. 33, page 12), determine (1) the size of the individual diamonds, (2) the number of rows within the eight star points, and (3) the size of the squares between the star points, or if the Lone Star is to be made into a rectangular shape, the size of the base triangles between four of the star points.

The size of the setting squares between the star points can be determined after the whole star has been sewn unless the squares are design blocks. Measure a finished diamond row inside a star point as the outer edges may have been stretched.

When the Lone Star is used with four squares and four base triangles, the long side of the base triangle is equal to the diagonal of the corner square (Fig. 34). To find the diagonal, multiply the measurement of the setting square by 1.414. Add 1¼" for seam allowances to determine the size of square to cut to make the base triangle (Fig. 34). Cut the square diagonally twice (Fig. 35).

MEASURING THE DIAMOND

Diamond measurements are described by degree and width. To measure the size of the Lone Star, the length of the sides must also be measured: 1½" width = length of side of 2⅛"; 2" width = length of side of 2⅞"; 2½" width = length of side of 3½"; and 3" width = length of side of 4¼". (Fig. 36).

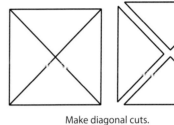

Make diagonal cuts.

Fig. 35. Base triangles for Lone Star blocks

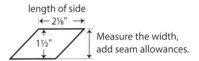

length of side
|← 2⅛" →|
1½"
Measure the width, add seam allowances.

Fig. 36. Determine width of strips.

Make a Lone Star without a pattern

★ Select a diamond size such as the 2" diamond.

★ Measure the sides of the diamond (2⅞") or 2.875")

★ Decide if the star points will have five or six rows of stars. Let's assume five.

★ Multiply 2.875" x 5 = 14.375", which is the size of the corner square (sides of diamonds x number of rows).

★ The base triangle is 1.414 x the corner square. Multiply 14.375" x 1.414 = 20.326".

★ Add two corners plus one base triangle to find the size of the square that will encompass the Lone Star. Add 14.375" + 20.326" = 14.375" = 49.076" or a 49" square.

★ Cut 2½" strips of fabric for the strata that will finish as 2" diamonds.

★ Cut 45-degree, 2½" wide slices from the five layer strata.

★ Lay out five 45-degree slices for each star point.

★ Sew the slices into star point pairs, then quarters, then halves and finally the whole.

★ Measure a star point from tip-to-tip to find the size of the corner square. Multiply the side of the corner square by 1.414 to find the size of the base triangle and add 1¼" to the result. Cut the square diagonally twice.

★ Set in the corners and base triangles. Add borders to make a double comforter that measures 76" x 86".

CHINOOK, 61" x 61", designed and pieced by the author and quilted by Vi Russell

CHINOOK

1 Lone Star block
8 Chinook blocks, 10⅝"

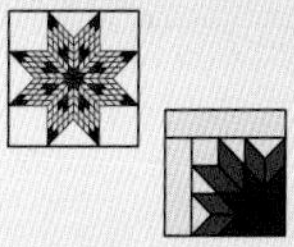

★ ★ ★
**Strip-pieced
Lone Star
p. 16**

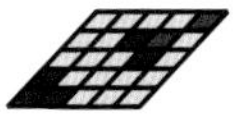

Cut strips selvage to selvage. Be sure to label all your pieces with their cut sizes.

Materials	Yards	First cut		Second cut	
Light Gray	2				
Lone Star		18 strips	2"	strip piecing	
Chinook blocks	1 strip	5½"	4 squares	5½"	
		1 strip	3"	8 squares	3"
		1 strip	2⅝"	8 squares	2⅝"
		2 strips	2⅝"	8 rectangles	2⅝" x 9"
		3 strips	2⅝"	8 rectangles	2⅝" x 11⅛"
Black	2½				
Lone Star		5 strips	2"	strip piecing	
(background)		1 piece	36" x 65"	(see wedges, page 20)	
Chinook blocks	2 strips	2"	strip piecing		
		1 strip	5⅛"	4 squares	5⅛"
Red	1¾				
Lone Star		2 strips	2"	strip piecing	
Chinook blocks	4 strips	2"	strip piecing		
Border		6 strips	4½"	strip piecing	
Binding		1 rectangle	18" x 42"		
Border print	½	6 strips	1½"		
Backing	3⅝	2 panels	33" x 65"		
Batting		65" x 65"			

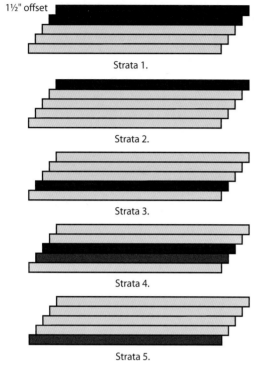

1½" offset

Strata 1.

Strata 2.

Strata 3.

Strata 4.

Strata 5.

Fig. 37. Sew strata using 2" x 42" strips.

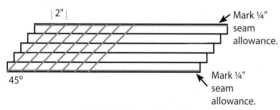

| 2" |

Mark ¼" seam allowance.

45°

Mark ¼" seam allowance.

Fig. 38. Trim and cut slices.

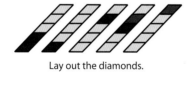

Lay out the diamonds.

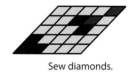

Sew diamonds.

Fig. 39. Lay out and sew diamonds.

Fig. 37–39. Lone Star

BLOCK ASSEMBLY

It is important to cut, sew, and press carefully when working with diamonds because of the bias edges. It is also important that the small diamonds and the large diamond star points are the correct measurements before the star is assembled so the Chinook blocks and black background pieces will fit the star.

Each layer in the 5" layer strata must measure 1½" finished.

Lone Star

Note that, for the small diamonds, each of the 5 different strip combinations (strata sets) contains five strips 2" wide. To maximize the number of diamonds you can cut from a strata set, off-set each strip 1½", forming a stair-stepped 45-degree angle. Make the five strata sets as shown in Fig. 37.

★ Trim off the stair steps to make a 45-degree beginning cut. Mark ¼" seam allowances along the top and bottom diamonds in each row. Cut eight 45-degree 2"-wide slices from each of the five strata sets (Fig. 38).

★ Arrange the five 45-degree slices into eight identical large diamonds with each diamond having five rows of small diamonds (Fig. 39).

★ Place the slices right sides together and match the individual seams of each of the diamonds. Sew the five slices together in order (Fig. 39). Press carefully.

★ To assemble the star points, place two large diamonds right sides together. Sew the large diamonds into pairs (Fig. 40). Place two pairs right sides together and sew the pairs into halves (Fig. 41).

★ Match the centers of the two halves and pin. Baste the seam intersections at the center (Fig. 42). Open the halves to verify that the center seams match. Proceed to sew the halves into one whole star (Fig. 43).

Fig. 40. Sew two diamonds together.

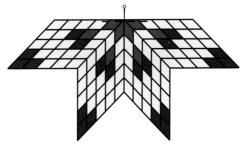

Fig. 42. Pin and baste half stars.

Fig. 41. Sew the pairs into half stars.

Fig. 43. Sew the halves.

Fig. 44. Whole star

Fig. 40–44. Lone Star, continued

2"

Fig. 45. Sew two red/black strips.

baste →

Fig. 46. Baste along the black edges.

45° 2⅜"

Fig. 47. Draw 45-degree angled lines.

Fig. 48. Sew, cut on drawn line.

Fig. 49. Pick out the stitches in the "V".

5½" square

Fig. 50. Cut square diagonally.

Fig. 51. Sew the base triangle to the chevron.

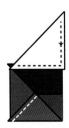 

Fig. 52. Sew the base triangle to the chevron.

Fig. 45–52. Chevron units

Chinook blocks

The Chinook blocks that lie between the star points finish 10⅝".

CHEVRON UNITS

★ Sew a 2" black strip and a 2" red strip together lengthwise (Fig. 45). Make two black/red strip-sets. Press the seam allowance of one set toward the black strip. Press the seam allowance of the second set toward the red strip.

★ With right sides together, machine baste the edges of the black/red strip-sets along the black edges (Fig. 46). Press. (Do not press open.)

★ Draw – do not cut – 45-degree parallel lines every 2⅜" across the strips (Fig. 47). With a ¼" seam allowance, sew across the strips to the right of each drawn line (Fig. 48). Cut on the drawn lines. Cut a total of 16 units.

★ Pick out the row of basting stitches at the top of the black strips. Open the double-V chevrons. Pick out the stitches in the seam allowance at the inside point of the "V" (Fig. 49).

★ Cut the four gray 5½" squares twice diagonally for the base triangles (Fig. 50). With right sides together, match and sew the black/red chevrons to the 16 gray base triangles, as follows: Match the legs of the chevrons to the 45-degree angles of the base triangles (Fig. 51). Stitch from the bottom of the triangle to the peak. Match and stitch the second leg to the adjacent side of the base triangle (Fig. 52). Sew all 16 units. Set the chevron units aside.

PARALLELOGRAM UNITS

★ Sew two red 2" strips together lengthwise (Fig. 53). Do not press open. Cut eight 45-degree 2⅝" slices from the layered red strips (Fig. 54). Press the parallelogram pairs open.

★ Straddle the corner of each of the 16 gray 2⅝" squares with a pair of red parallelograms (Fig. 55). Stitch in place with a ¼" seam allowance.

★ Cut the eight gray 3" squares in half diagonally (Fig. 56). Stitch a triangle to each side of the parallelogram pairs to make a 4¾" square (Fig. 57).

★ Sew a chevron unit to each side of a parallelogram unit (Fig. 58). Sew the two chevron units together like mitering a corner.

★ Cut the four black 5⅛" squares in half diagonally to make eight triangles (Fig. 59). Sew a triangle to the chevron side of each block. Press and trim the blocks to 9" (unfinished).

★ Sew a 2⅝" x 9" gray rectangle to the left edge of each Chinook block. Sew the remaining 2⅝" x 11⅛" rectangles as shown in the block assembly (Fig. 60) to complete the Chinook block. Make eight blocks.

3" square

Fig. 56. Cut squares diagonally.

Fig. 57. Stitch triangles to sides of parallelogram pairs.

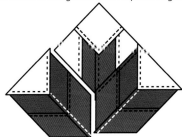

Fig. 58. Sew a chevron unit to each side of parallelogram unit.

5⅛" square

Fig. 59. Cut square diagonally.

Fig. 53–59. Parallelogram units

2"

Fig. 53. Sew red strips.

45° 2⅝" 2⅝"

Fig. 54. Cut 45-degree slices.

2⅝" square

Fig. 55. Sew parallelogram pair to square.

Fig. 53–55. Parallelogram units

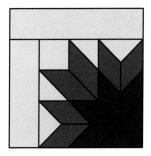

Fig. 60. Block assembly

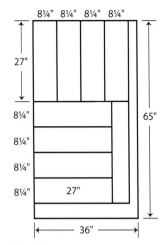

Fig. 61. Wedge cutting diagram.

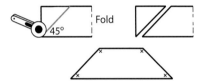

Fig. 62. Trim and mark wedges.

Fig. 63. Sew the wedge to the top of square.

Fig. 61–63. Wedges

Quilt assembly

★ Sew the eight (unfinished) 11⅛" Chinook blocks between the star points, as shown in Fig. 66, page 21, in the following manner: Sew from the bottom of the inside "V" to the marked seam allowance at the tip of the large diamond. Repeat for the other side of the block. Sew all eight Chinook blocks to the star. Press the seam allowances toward the blocks.

Wedges

Use the following directions to cut the black background wedges to keep the grain of the fabric the same in all the wedges. Mark each wedge as horizontal or vertical on the wrong side of the fabric as each rectangle is cut.

★ To cut the wedges from the black 36" x 65" (slightly oversized) piece, first cut a 27"-length of the fabric, as shown in the wedge cutting diagram (Fig. 61). Cut this strip into four vertical 8¼" x 27" pieces. Cut a 27"-wide strip parallel to the selvages. Cut this strip into four horizontal 8¼" x 27" pieces (Fig. 61).

★ Fold the eight rectangles in half, matching the short ends. Cut away a 45-degree triangle from the end of each folded rectangle. The wedges that remain include seam allowances (Fig. 62).

★ Mark the seam allowance intersections at each corner of the eight wedges. Sew the tops of the wedges to the Chinook blocks that point to the corners of the quilt (Fig. 63). (Do not sew into the seam allowances.) Next, sew one angled side of each wedge to the adjacent Chinook block on point (Fig. 64). Continue sewing the horizontal and vertical wedges to the Chinook block. Finally, miter the wedges together at the corners (Fig. 65).

★ For the red border, use a bias seam to sew the six 4½" strips, end-to-end, to make the lengths needed for the quilt. Sew the 1½" print border strips together and cut to size.

★ Sew a red border strip to a print border strip lengthwise. Repeat for the other border strips. Treat the combined strips as one. Sew the borders to the quilt with the print border on the outside and miter the corners.

FINISHING

Layer the quilt with batting and a backing, then quilt the layers. Bind the raw edges of the quilt with 2" continuous, double-fold bias binding.

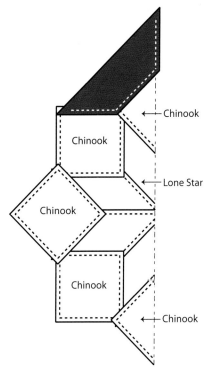

Fig. 65. Miter the wedges at the corner.

Fig. 65. Wedges

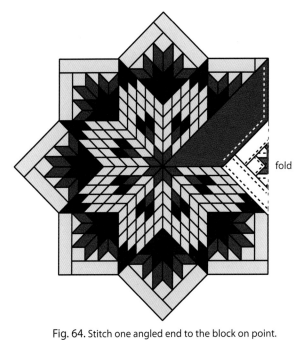

Fig. 64. Stitch one angled end to the block on point.

Fig. 64. Wedges

Fig. 66. Quilt assembly

The two most common Log Cabin block designs, Log Cabin and Courthouse Steps, both have a central square, which can vary in size. In the traditional Log Cabin (Fig. 67), rectangular strips are added in a clockwise or counter-clockwise direction. Each strip overlaps the last applied strip. In Courthouse Steps, the strips are added in the sequence of top, bottom, side, side, etc. (Fig. 68).

Both Log Cabin block designs begin with a square and finish as a square. When the technique of sewing strips (logs) to a central geometric figure other than a square is used, more design possibilities can occur. The term "Log Cabin," as used here, refers to the construction technique rather than the block design itself.

When the Log Cabin technique is used to sew 45- or 60-degree diamonds, a Log Cabin star can be produced. Large over-all designs like the Lone Star can be made with Log Cabin diamonds. The color and design variations are determined according to the values and arrangements of the logs within the diamonds.

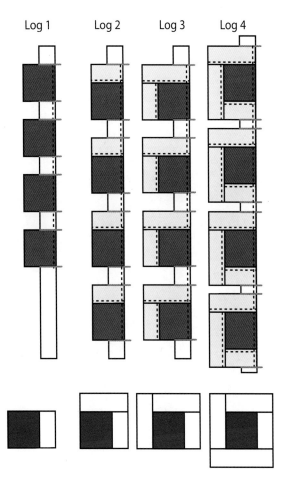

Fig. 67. Traditional Log Cabin

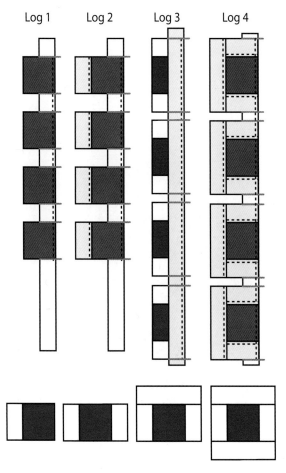

Fig. 68. Courthouse Steps

The star, as a design component of the Log Cabin block, is illustrated in the LOG CABIN STAR quilt, page 26. The quilt design includes the classic Aunt Eliza's Star, which is sewn Log Cabin-style (Fig. 69–76). The Aunt Eliza's Star is then set within the traditional Log Cabin block, which is cut diagonally and re-sewn to produce the new four-block star.

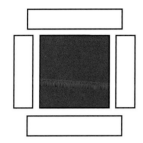

Fig. 69. Chain piece the logs to the center square.

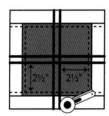

Fig. 70. Cut the block into quarters, 2¼" from seam line.

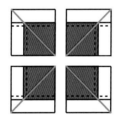

Fig. 71. Draw lines from the corners to the center.

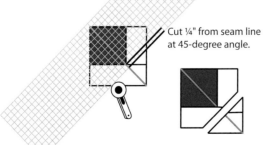

Cut ¼" from seam line at 45-degree angle.

Fig. 72. Cut away the corners.

Fig. 69–76. Aunt Eliza's Star block

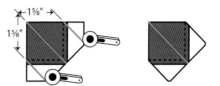

Fig. 73. Trim the corners 1⅝" from drawn line to make star-point units.

3¼" square

Fig. 74. Cut squares twice on the diagonal.

Fig. 75. Sew triangles to sides of the star-point units.

3¼" square

Fig. 76. Block assembly

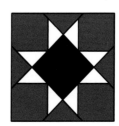

Another option is to cut a foundation-pieced Log Cabin Pineapple block to create a traditional Delectable Mountain block to surround the stars (Fig. 77–85). A second technique for Delectable Mountain uses half-squares for the quilt border (Fig. 87, page 25).

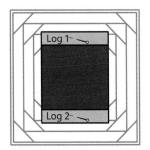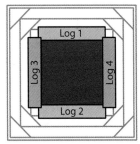

Fig. 81. Stitch Log 2 to opposite side; sew Logs 3 and 4.

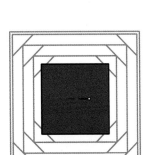

Fig. 77. Pin square to foundation.

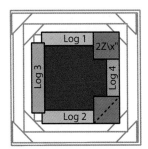

Fig. 82. Place a square even with the edges of the logs.

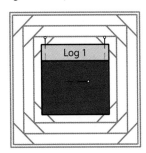

Fig. 78. Align Log 1 with edge of center square.

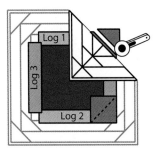

Fig. 83. Turn to the right side, fold the foundation away from the sewn corner. Trim the square and logs.

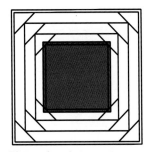

Fig. 79. Turn foundation over, sew on line.

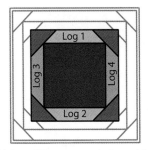

Fig. 84. Sew all four corners, before adding next round of logs.

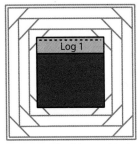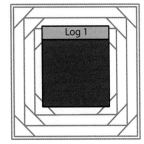

Fig. 80. Turn block to right side, press Log 1.

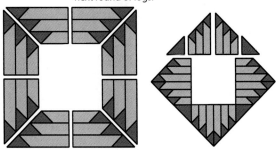

Fig. 85. Cut block horizontally, vertically, and on both diagonals.

Fig. 77–85. Delectable Mountain block

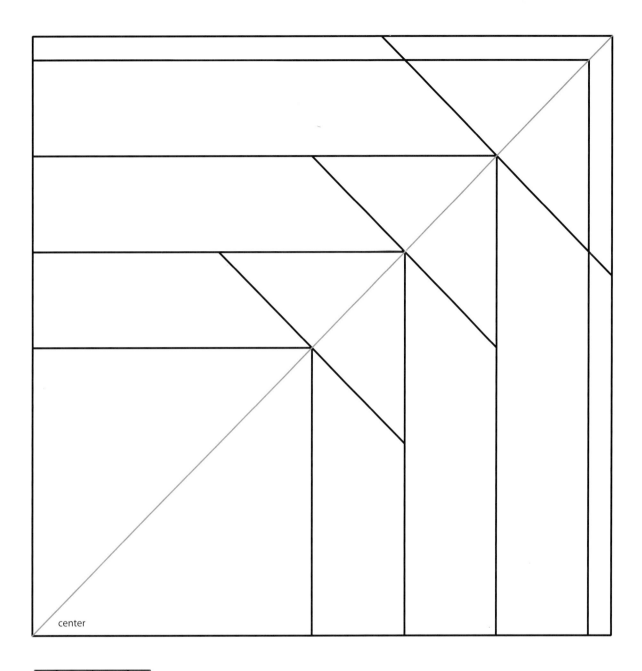

center

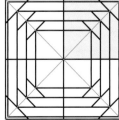

Fig. 86. Full-size foundation for ¼ Log Cabin Pineapple-block for the Delectable Mountain block.

a b c d   d c b a

Fig. 87. Delectable Mountain border uses half-squares.

LOG CABIN STAR, 90" x 106½", made by Lella King and quilted by Gloria Badgett.

LOG CABIN STAR

36 Log Cabin Stars, 15¼"

★ ★ ★
**Log Cabin
star points p. 29**

Cut strips selvage to selvage. Be sure to label all your pieces with their cut sizes.

Materials	Yards	First cut		Second cut	
White	2¾				
Log Cabin Star					
centers		4 strips	9¾"	36 squares	9¾"
base triangles	5 strips	7¼"	30 squares	7¼"	
Aunt Eliza's Stars					
star point units	7 strips	1½"	132 rectangles	1½" x 5½"	
star point units	5 strips	1½"	132 rectangles	1½" x 7½"	
Dark teal	2¼				
Log Cabin Star					
base triangles	5 strips	7¼"	6 squares	7¼"	
Border strips		14 strips	2¾"		
Log Cabin logs					
Light					
log 1	½	9 strips	1½"	36 rectangles	1½" x 9¾"
log 2	½	12 strips	1½"	36 rectangles	1½" x 10¾"
log 3	½	12 strips	1½"	36 rectangles	1½" x 10¾"
log 4	½	12 strips	1½"	36 rectangles	1½" x 11¾"
Medium					
log 5	⅝	12 strips	1½"	36 rectangles	1½" x 11¾"
log 6	⅝	12 strips	1½"	36 rectangles	1½" x 12¾"
log 7	⅝	12 strips	1½"	36 rectangles	1½" x 12¾"
log 8	⅝	12 strips	1½"	36 rectangles	1½" x 13¾"
Dark					
log 9	⅝	12 strips	1½"	36 rectangles	1½" x 13¾"
log 10	⅞	18 strips	1½"	36 rectangles	1½" x 14¾"
log 11	⅞	18 strips	1½"	36 rectangles	1½" x 14¾"
log 12	¾	18 strips	1½"	36 rectangles	1½" x 15¾"
Teal	2¼				
Aunt Eliza's Stars					
star point units	10 strips	5½"	66 squares	5½"	
base triangles	6 strips	3¼"	66 squares	3¼"	
Blue green	⅝				
Aunt Eliza's Stars					
centers		6 strips	3½"	66 squares	(use template)
Backing	8	3 panels	37½" x 94"		
Binding	½				
Batting		94" x 110½"			

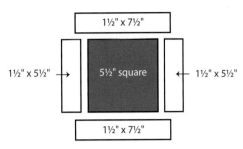

Fig. 88. Chain piece logs to the center square.

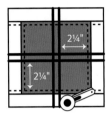

Fig. 89. Cut block into quarters, 2¼" from seam line.

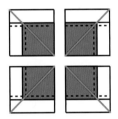

Fig. 90. Draw lines from the corners to the center.

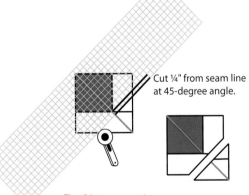

Fig. 91. Cut away the corners.

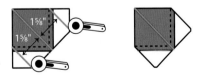

Fig. 92. Trim the corners 1⅝" from drawn line to make star-point units.

Fig. 88–92. Aunt Eliza's Star block

BLOCK ASSEMBLY

Aunt Eliza's Star

The star point units for the Aunt Eliza's Star blocks begin as Courthouse Steps blocks with only one log on each side.

- ★ Chain-piece the 1½" x 5½" white logs to opposite sides of the 5½" teal squares (Fig. 88). Sew the 1½" x 7½" logs to the remaining sides of the squares to complete the 66 blocks.

- ★ Turn the bordered squares to the wrong side. Place the 2¼" line of the ruler on one seam line that joins a log to the square. Cut across the square. Repeat this cut on all four sides to quarter the block (Fig. 89). Scraps between the quarters will remain after cutting. Draw lines on the wrong side from the corners to the center (Fig. 90).

- ★ Where the logs overlap, cut off the corners of the units, leaving a ¼" seam allowance beyond the teal point, as follows: Align the 45-degree line of the rotary ruler with the seam line. Position the cutting edge ¼" from the corner of the teal square to allow for the seam allowance. Cut away the corner (Fig. 91).

- ★ Next, cut away the corners adjacent to the just cut edge, as follows: On the back of the unit, measure 1⅝" from the drawn mid line as shown in (Fig. 92). Cut off one side of the unit. Repeat for the other side. Cut all the star point units this way.

- ★ Cut 66 teal 3¼" squares twice on the diagonal to make the base triangles for the Aunt Eliza's Stars (Fig. 93).

- ★ For each star, sew star point units to opposite sides of the 3¼" blue-green center squares as shown in the block assembly, page 30.

- ★ Sew a base triangle to both sides of two other units (Fig. 94). Sew these to the two remaining sides of the center square to complete the star.

Log Cabin Stars

The Log Cabin star point units are made from Log Cabin blocks cut in quarters.

★ Use Log Cabin piecing in a clockwise direction to chain piece the logs to 36 white 9¾" squares (Fig. 96). The squares will have three logs on each side when complete.

★ Spray the Log Cabin blocks with fabric sizing to avoid stretching the bias cut edges created in the next steps.

★ On the wrong side of the 15¼" unfinished blocks, draw a 6½" wide X from corner to corner, as follows: Center the 3¼" line of the ruler on one diagonal pair of corners. Draw a line. Then rotate the square to measure and draw the opposite side of the 6½"-wide diagonal (Fig. 97). Draw the second 6½"-wide diagonal to complete the X.

★ Cut the 6½"-wide X from the Log Cabin leaving a 6½" square on point and four base triangles as scrap (Fig. 98, page 30).

★ Cut the 7¼" white squares and the 7¼" dark teal squares twice diagonally to make new base triangles for the Log Cabin Star blocks (Fig. 99).

★ Lay out each unit of the block. Replace the original white square on point with an on-point Aunt Eliza's Star. Replace the Log Cabin's base triangle with two white and/or dark teal triangles. (The blocks at the edges of the quilt will have one dark teal base triangles or two dark teal triangles if the block is a corner block.)

★ Sew two Log Cabin star point units to opposite sides of the new Aunt's Eliza's Star center as shown in the block assembly diagram.

★ Sew two white and/or teal base triangles to each side of two Log Cabin units. Sew these units to the block. Make 36 Log Cabin Star blocks.

3¼" square

Fig. 93. Cut squares twice on the diagonal.

Fig. 94. Sew triangles to sides of the star-point units.

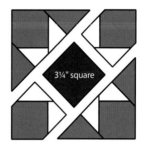 

3¼" square

Fig. 95. Block assembly

Fig. 93–95. Aunt Eliza's Star block, continued

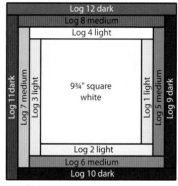

Fig. 96. Piece Log Cabin block.

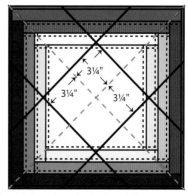

Fig. 97. Draw lines for the Log Cabin star points.

Fig. 96–97. Log Cabin Star points

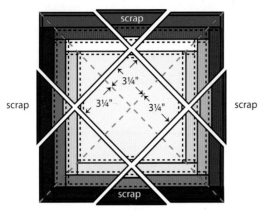

Fig. 98. Cut on the drawn lines.

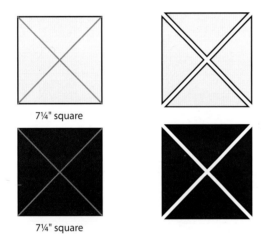

7¼" square

7¼" square

Fig. 99. Cut squares to make base triangles.

QUILT ASSEMBLY

★ Sew the star blocks into four-block units (Fig. 100). Sew three of the four-block units across and three down to make the quilt body.

★ Use bias seams to sew the 2¾" dark teal border strips, end-to-end, as needed to make two 92" lengths and four 96½" lengths.

★ Sew a 96½" dark teal border strip to each side of the quilt body. Sew two 96½" strips to the top and bottom of the quilt.

★ Sew the remaining 30 Aunt Eliza's Stars into two rows of 15 stars for the borders at the top and at the bottom of the quilt. Sew the star borders to the quilt.

★ Sew a 96½" dark teal strip to the top and bottom to complete the quilt top.

FINISHING

Layer the quilt with batting and a backing, then quilt the layers. Bind the raw edges of the quilt with 2" continuous, double-fold bias binding.

Block assembly

Fig. 98–99. Log Cabin Stars, continued

Fig. 100. Quilt assembly

More AQS Books

This is only a small selection of the books available from the American Quilter's Society. AQS books are known worldwide for timely topics, clear writing, beautiful color photos, and accurate illustrations and patterns. The following books are available from your local bookseller, quilt shop, or public library.

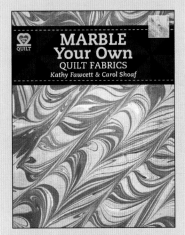

#1298

#1302

#1275

#1280

#1281

#1279

#1282

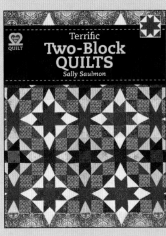

#1283

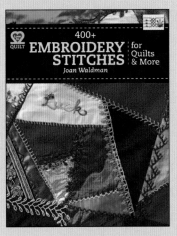

#1274

LOOK for these books nationally.
CALL or **VISIT** our website at

1-800-626-5420
www.AmericanQuilter.com